ARCHAEOLOGICAL MYSTERIES

SECRETS OF
MESA VERDE

CLIFF DWELLINGS OF THE PUEBLO

BY GAIL FAY

Consultant:
Benjamin R. Kracht, PhD
Professor of Anthropology
Chair, Department of Cherokee and Indigenous Studies
Northeastern State University
Tahlequah, Oklahoma

CAPSTONE PRESS
a capstone imprint

Edge Books are published by Capstone Press,
1710 Roe Crest Drive, North Mankato, Minnesota 56003
www.capstonepub.com

Library of Congress Cataloging-in-Publication Data
Fay, Gail.
 Secrets of Mesa Verde : cliff dwellings of the pueblo / by Gail Fay.
    pages cm.—(Edge Books. Archaeological mysteries)
 Includes bibliographical references and index.
Summary: "Describes the archeological wonder of Mesa Verde, including
discovery, artifacts, ancient peoples, and preservation"—Provided by publisher.
 ISBN 978-1-4765-9918-2 (library binding)
 ISBN 978-1-4765-9927-4 (paperback)
 ISBN 978-1-4765-9923-6 (eBook pdf)
 1. Pueblo Indians—Colorado—Mesa Verde National Park—Antiquities—Juvenile
literature. 2. Cliff-dwellings--Colorado--Mesa Verde National Park—Juvenile
literature. 3. Mesa Verde National Park (Colo.)—Antiquities—Juvenile literature.
I. Title.
E99.P9F375 2015
978.8'27—dc23

2014006969

Developed and Produced by Focus Strategic Communications, Inc.
    Adrianna Edwards: project manager
    Ron Edwards: editor
    Rob Scanlan: designer and compositor
    Karen Hunter: media researcher
    Francine Geraci: copy editor and proofreader
    Wendy Scavuzzo: fact checker

TABLE OF CONTENTS

CHAPTER 1   A CITY OF STONE 4

CHAPTER 2   DIGGING UP MESA VERDE 8

CHAPTER 3   THE ANCESTRAL PUEBLOANS 14

CHAPTER 4   MESA VERDE ABANDONED 22

CHAPTER 5   PROTECTING MESA VERDE 26

GLOSSARY 30

READ MORE 31

CRITICAL THINKING USING THE COMMON CORE 31

INTERNET SITES 32

INDEX 32

CHAPTER ONE

A CITY OF STONE

On a cold morning in December 1888, two cowboys set off on horseback. They were searching for lost cattle in southwest Colorado. As the men rode, snow began to fall. They could not see very far ahead.

The area had many steep cliffs. Richard Wetherill and Charles Mason did not want to fall over a cliff, so they got off their horses and started

Charles Mason

Richard Wetherill

walking. They came to the edge of a **mesa** and looked across the canyon. The men could not believe what they saw. In an **alcove** under the mesa top was a city made of stone. They had found Mesa Verde!

ARCHAEOLOGICAL FACT

In Spanish Mesa Verde means "green table." Spanish explorers may have used the name to describe the flat-topped hills that were covered with green trees.

Richard Wetherill and Charles Mason found cliff dwellings in December 1888. Wetherill named one of them Cliff Palace.

flat-topped hills of Mesa Verde

mesa—a broad hill with a flat top and steep sides

alcove—a large, arched recession formed in a cliff wall

MESA VERDE'S FIRST EXPLORERS

Wetherill and Mason climbed down the cliff to take a look around. At the alcove's opening, they found big circular buildings that were sunk into the ground. They looked like stone pits. There were many small rooms behind these pits. The men also found tall towers and high walls that reached up to the alcove's ceiling. Many of the rooms contained the remains of sandals, baskets, and ceramic pots. It was as if people had suddenly left and forgotten their belongings. But why did they leave? And where did they go?

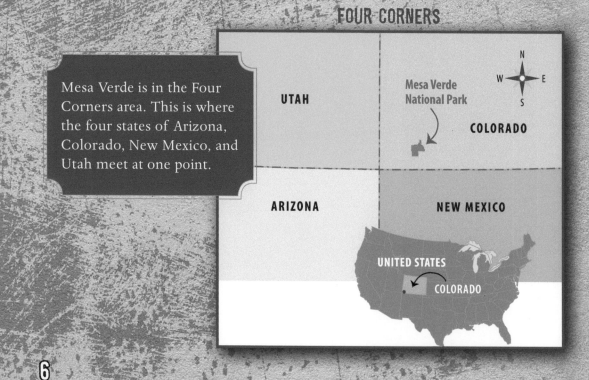

FOUR CORNERS

Mesa Verde is in the Four Corners area. This is where the four states of Arizona, Colorado, New Mexico, and Utah meet at one point.

UTAH

Mesa Verde
National Park

COLORADO

ARIZONA

NEW MEXICO

UNITED STATES

COLORADO

Wetherill and Mason told many people about their amazing discovery. Soon **archaeologists** started exploring Mesa Verde. They wanted to learn about the people who had lived there. No one knew what the cliff dwellers called themselves. They did not leave written records about their history or **culture**. To find answers archaeologists began to study the dwellings and **artifacts** that these people left behind.

archaeologist—a scientist who studies how people lived in the past by analyzing their artifacts

culture—a people's way of life, ideas, art, customs, and traditions

artifact—an object used in the past that was made by people

WILLIAM HENRY JACKSON

Wetherill and Mason helped make Mesa Verde famous. But they were not the first to find the dwellings. William Henry Jackson took the first photograph of a Mesa Verde cliff dwelling. That was 14 years earlier, but for some reason his photos did not capture the public's attention at that time.

pioneer photographer
William Henry Jackson

CHAPTER TWO

DIGGING UP MESA VERDE

Archaeologists found 600 cliff dwellings in Mesa Verde. They are made of sandstone pieces held together with a mud mixture of soil, water, and ash. Most of the dwellings have only one to five rooms. But some are much bigger.

Cliff Palace is the largest cliff dwelling in Mesa Verde. It may have been a central meeting place. The palace has 150 rooms and 23 stone pits called **kivas**. Kivas were round underground rooms. The people may have used kivas for religious ceremonies and to keep warm in the winter. Each kiva had a fire pit in the floor. A vent let out the smoke.

kiva—an underground room that may have been used for special ceremonies

kiva

GUSTAF NORDENSKIÖLD

In 1891 Swedish scientist Gustaf Nordenskiöld studied and photographed Mesa Verde. He led the first full exploration of Cliff Palace and other dwellings. He also wrote the first scientific book on the dwellings. The book was called *The Cliff Dwellers of the Mesa Verde*. Nordenskiöld was only 23 at the time.

Gustaf Nordenskiöld's photo of Cliff Palace

MANY HOUSES, MANY ROOMS

Spruce Tree House has around 114 rooms and eight kivas. Each kiva roof has a square opening. People probably put a ladder through this opening so they could climb in and out. Spruce Tree House is the third largest cliff dwelling in Mesa Verde.

inside the kiva at Spruce Tree House

Archaeologists found many other cliff dwellings. They named three of them Balcony House, Square Tower House, and Long House. They also found similar stone and mud buildings on top of the mesa. Archaeologists think people lived on the mesa for 650 years before they moved to the cliffs.

ARCHAEOLOGICAL FACT

Each kiva had a sipapu. This was a hole in the floor. The cliff dwellers believed that their people came from the spirit world through this hole.

SIPAPU

the sipapu (small hole) next to the fire pit in a kiva

WHAT ARCHAEOLOGISTS FOUND

Artifacts can tell us a lot about cliff dwellers—what they ate, wore, and used every day. At Mesa Verde, archaeologists found items such as baskets, pottery, tools, shoes, clothing, and jewelry. Many of these items were found in the rooms and in the open spaces. In Cliff Palace, archaeologists found corn cobs stuck in a plastered wall.

Bones can also teach us about cliff dwellers. Archaeologists found human skeletons in trash heaps and burial rooms at Mesa Verde. The skeletons show that the men stood about 5 feet, 4 inches (163 centimeters) tall. The women were about 5 feet (152 cm) tall. The skeletons also showed that most cliff dwellers lived only until they were in their early 30s.

Baskets found at Mesa Verde were likely used daily by the cliff dwellers.

RED PAINTINGS

Archaeologists found two red paintings inside the square tower at Cliff Palace. One painting is a rectangle with eight zigzag lines inside. The other shows four tall lines. Each line has many short lines sticking out of one side. Archaeologists think the paintings show how the moon moves across the sky.

a red painting found at Cliff Palace

CHAPTER THREE

THE ANCESTRAL PUEBLOANS

For hundreds of years, archaeologists used the term "Anasazi" to describe the cliff dwellers. Today archaeologists prefer the term "Ancestral Puebloans." The scientists studied the buildings and artifacts. Then they began to figure out who the cliff dwellers were. They were **ancestors** of the Pueblo people. Today Pueblo people live in New Mexico and Arizona.

The Ancestral Puebloans moved to the Mesa Verde area around AD 500. They decided to leave their **nomadic** ways. They settled on top of the mesa. There the soil was good for farming. Archaeologists found **farming terraces** on the mesa top. These steps trapped rainwater in the flat sections where seeds were planted. The Ancestral Puebloans probably grew corn, beans, and squash in these terraces.

Farming terraces are still used today.

At first the Ancestral Puebloans lived in pithouses. They dug shallow pits in the ground. Then they made roofs of wood covered with mud. Around 700 they started building rows of attached homes. These were called pueblos. The pueblos had flat roofs made of stone, mud, and wood beams called vigas.

ancestor—a member of a person's family who lived a long time ago

nomadic—traveling from place to place in search of food and water

farming terrace—a wide step built into a hillside so that people can farm in the flat sections

a pithouse

MOVE TO THE CLIFFS

Between 1200 and 1250, most of the Ancestral Puebloans started leaving the mesa top. They moved to the alcoves below. They built the same pueblo homes in the cliffs. But they needed to strengthen the walls. So they stuck small pieces of stone into the mud mixture.

In many ways life was harder in the cliffs. The Ancestral Puebloans had to carry tree trunks down the steep cliffs to build their homes. They still farmed on the mesa top. So they had to climb up the steep cliffs to reach their crops.

Sticking stones into the mud for building support is called chinking. The stones in the mud of the Mesa Verde cliff dwellings are still visible.

So why did the Ancestral Puebloans move? Some historians think they moved to be safe from enemy attacks. Many cliff dwellings have tall towers. These could have been used for shooting arrows at enemies. Others think the Ancestral Puebloans moved because the mesa became too crowded. Maybe families began to fight with one another. Maybe the soil became overworked and less **fertile**. By moving to the cliffs, the Ancestral Puebloans would have had more land for farming.

fertile—having many nutrients

ARCHAEOLOGICAL FACT

The Mesa Verde ranges from around 6,800 to 8,570 feet (2,073 to 2,612 meters) above sea level. Summers are hot and dry, while winters are cold and snowy.

DAILY LIFE IN THE CLIFFS

Life was very hard for the Ancestral Puebloans. Even so, they lived in the cliffs for about 100 years. They farmed corn and other crops. Archaeologists found flat grindstones at Spruce Tree House. Women probably spent hours each day grinding corn into flour to make a thin bread called piki. The cliff dwellers also hunted rabbits. They gathered nuts, berries, and seeds. They built small rooms at the back of the alcoves. This is where they stored dried food.

The Ancestral Puebloans used flat grindstones for grinding corn.

Human skulls found at Mesa Verde have worn-down teeth. The Ancestral Puebloans ground their corn on sandstone. Archaeologists think that bits of stone ended up in their food. Chewing the stone probably wore down their teeth.

Archaeologists found turkey bones. The cliff dwellers probably raised turkeys in pens at the back of the alcoves. They used turkey bones for necklaces. They used the feathers to make blankets and cloaks for the cold winters.

daily life at Mesa Verde

WATER

The Ancestral Puebloans needed water for drinking and farming. They figured out ways to trap rain and melted snow. At Mesa Verde archaeologists found four large, shallow holes. They were probably used as tanks to store water for dry seasons.

a storage tank in Mesa Verde

The Ancestral Puebloans also stored water in clay jars. They were well known for their black-on-white pottery designs. Scientists believe faraway tribes may have traded seashells for the Ancestral Puebloans' pottery. Perhaps that is why seashells were found in Mesa Verde, which is 800 miles (1,287 kilometers) away from the nearest ocean.

PUEBLOAN POTTERY

The Ancestral Puebloans made pottery for hundreds of years. Black paint was used on white clay to create special designs. Shapes such as parallel lines, triangles, and dots were painted on the light-colored clay. The clay was formed into shapes by hand. Then it was hardened using fire. This made the pottery strong and protected the contents. Today pottery is still made the same way.

The black paint came from boiled plants or from crushed rock that had iron in it.

CHAPTER FOUR

MESA VERDE
ABANDONED

By 1250 thousands of Ancestral Puebloans lived in Mesa Verde. Then they began to leave their dwellings. By 1300 the entire area was deserted. We may never know for sure why the Ancestral Puebloans suddenly left their cliff dwellings. It is one of history's mysteries. But there are several theories.

Many experts believe that a **drought** forced the Ancestral Puebloans to move. Tree rings show that a severe drought happened in the Mesa Verde area between 1275 and 1300. Crops could not grow without rain, and this could have led to a shortage of food.

The Ancestral Puebloans may have left because of enemy attacks. However, the skeletons show little proof of this. Or perhaps the cliff dwellings became too crowded. There may have been fighting between families over food and water. It was common for ancient people to move on when resources became scarce.

drought—a long period of weather with little or no rainfall

TREE RING DATING

Scientists use tree rings to find out when events happened in the past. Each year a tree's trunk gains a new growth ring. At Mesa Verde scientists removed pieces from wood beams in the cliff dwellings. They counted the rings to find out the age of the trees when they were cut down and used to build the dwellings. Tree rings showed evidence of drought in Mesa Verde. Thin rings close together indicate little rainfall and slow growth. Wide rings show heavier rainfall and good growth.

Archaeologists use special hollow drills to collect narrow, cylindrical wood samples from old trees at Mesa Verde.

WHERE DID THEY GO?

For many years people thought the Ancestral Puebloans just disappeared. Some people even believed that they were kidnapped by aliens! Archaeologists today believe the cliff dwellers simply **migrated** to the south. The cliff dwellers may have moved to the less crowded areas along the Rio Grande. Today many modern Puebloans still live in these parts of Arizona and New Mexico.

migrate—to move from one place to another

ARCHAEOLOGICAL FACT

The rumor of alien kidnappings began with an episode of the TV show *X-Files*. The characters on the show wondered if the Ancestral Puebloans had actually been abducted by aliens. Some people confused this fictional TV story with reality. Visitors still ask park rangers about these alien abductions.

The cliff dwellings remained hidden because they were surrounded by a forest.

Some people wonder why it took more than 500 years to find the cliff dwellings. Gustaf Nordenskiöld was not surprised it took this long. In his book Nordenskiöld said the forest around Mesa Verde was like a maze. So people would need luck to find the dwellings. Many boulders blocked the way to the dwellings, and the cliffs were steep.

Steep cliffs made it difficult to find the dwellings of the Ancestral Puebloans.

CHAPTER FIVE

PROTECTING
MESA VERDE

When Richard Wetherill came upon Cliff Palace, he knew he had found something special. His family felt the same way. In 1889 Wetherill's father wrote a letter to the Smithsonian Institution in Washington, D.C. He wanted the organization to protect the Mesa Verde cliff dwellings. He was worried people might steal the artifacts or destroy the buildings.

In 1900 Virginia McClurg and Lucy Peabody started the Colorado Cliff Dwellings Association. They wanted to protect the Mesa Verde area. They also tried to make Mesa Verde a national park. They began to write letters and raise money.

ARCHAEOLOGICAL FACT

More than 500,000 people visit Mesa Verde National Park each year. In 1906, the year the park opened, there were only 27 visitors. In 2011 the park had nearly 600,000 visitors.

In 1906 President Theodore Roosevelt made Mesa Verde a national park. It is the only national park created to protect the artifacts and buildings of an ancient people. Mesa Verde National Park protects 600 cliff dwellings and more than 3 million artifacts.

Theodore Roosevelt was known as "the conservation president."

VISITING MESA VERDE NATIONAL PARK TODAY

Mesa Verde National Park offers many things to do and see. On the mesa top, visitors can see pithouses at the Badger House Community. At the Far View sites, they can see pueblos. They can also see a farming terrace near the Cedar Tree Tower. Visitors can tour several cliff dwellings. The three most popular are Cliff Palace, Spruce Tree House, and Balcony House. The Chapin Mesa Archeological Museum has displays that show what life was like for the Ancestral Puebloans.

ARCHAEOLOGICAL FACT

The new Mesa Verde Visitor and Research Center opened in 2012. It has an exhibit on the modern Pueblo people of New Mexico and Arizona.

To protect the cliff dwellings, only a limited number of visitors are allowed daily. The dwellings are checked regularly for cracks. Sometimes crews have to repair the walls so the buildings do not collapse.

Archaeologists continue to study Mesa Verde. So far they have learned that the Ancestral Puebloans were skilled farmers, builders, and rock climbers. But there's so much more to learn about them just waiting to be discovered.

visitors at Cliff Palace

GLOSSARY

alcove (AL-kohv)—a large, arched recession formed in a cliff wall

ancestor (AN-ses-tuhr)—a member of a person's family who lived a long time ago

archaeologist (ar-kee-AH-luh-jist)—a scientist who studies how people lived in the past by analyzing their artifacts

artifact (AR-tuh-fact)—an object used in the past that was made by people

culture (KUHL-chuhr)—a people's way of life, ideas, art, customs, and traditions

drought (DROUT)—a long period of weather with little or no rainfall

farming terrace (FAHR-ming TER-iss)—a wide step built into a hillside so that people can farm in the flat sections

fertile (FUHR-tuhl)—having many nutrients

kiva (KEE-vuh)—an underground room that may have been used for special ceremonies

mesa (MEY-suh)—a broad hill with a flat top and steep sides

migrate (MYE-grate)—to move from one place to another

nomadic (noh-MAD-ik)—traveling from place to place in search of food and water

READ MORE

Collins, Terry. *The Mesa Verde Cliff Dwellers: An Isabel Soto Archaeology Adventure*. Graphic Expeditions. Mankato, Minn.: Capstone Press, 2010.

McHugh, Erin. *National Parks: A Kid's Guide to America's Parks, Monuments, and Landmarks*. Black Dog & Leventhal Publishers, Inc.: New York, 2012.

CRITICAL THINKING USING THE COMMON CORE

1. Some archaeologists feel that crowding caused many changes for the Ancestral Puebloans. What were the changes? Do you agree that crowding was a likely cause, or do you agree with another explanation? Why? (Key Ideas and Details)

2. Why is the section What Archaeologists Found on pages 12–13 significant? Which of the scientists' findings seems to have provided the most information? Support your answer by including details from the section. (Key Ideas and Details)

3. Reread pages 22–24 and think about theories why the Ancient Puebloans left Mesa Verde. What do you think is the author's opinion? Why? What details in the text make you think that? (Integration of Knowledge and Ideas)

INTERNET SITES

FactHound offers a safe, fun way to find Internet sites related to this book. All of the sites on FactHound have been researched by our staff. Here's all you do:

Visit *www.facthound.com*

Type in this code: 9781476599182

INDEX

archaeologists, 7, 8, 11, 12, 13, 14, 18, 19, 20, 23, 24, 29

artifacts, 7, 12, 14, 26, 27

Balcony House, 11, 28

Chapin Mesa Archeological Museum, 28

Cliff Palace, 5, 8, 9, 12, 13, 26, 28

farming, 14, 16, 17, 18, 20, 22, 28, 29

Jackson, William Henry, 7

kivas, 8, 10, 11

Long House, 11

Mason, Charles, 4, 5, 6–7

McClurg, Virginia, 26

Nordenskiöld, Gustaf, 9, 25

Peabody, Lucy, 26

pithouses, 6, 15, 28

Roosevelt, Theodore, 27

Spruce Tree House, 10, 18, 28, 29

Square Tower House, 11

water, 8, 14, 20–21, 22

Wetherill, Richard, 4, 5, 6–7, 26